RADICA

VOL I

DRAMATIC TRUE LIFE STORIES

COMPILED & WRITTEN BY

JANET BALCOMBE

wildsidepublishing.com **WSP**

real stories. real hope.

Wild Side Publishing
PO Box 33, Ruawai 0530
Northland, New Zealand
wildsidepublishing.com
Telephone: +64 9 439 2713

© 2015 Janet Balcombe
Updated version printed February 2017

All rights reserved. No part of this publication may be reproduced, stored in a retrieval system or transmitted in any form or by any means electronic, mechanical, photocopying, recording or otherwise without the prior written permission of the publisher.

All stories contained herein are printed with the approval of people featured.

Some scripture quotations are taken from the Holy Bible, New International Version®, NIV®. Copyright ©1973, 1978, 1984, 2011 by Biblica, Inc.™ Used by permission of Zondervan. All rights reserved worldwide. www.zondervan.com The 'NIV' and 'New International Version' are trademarks registered in the United States Patent and Trademark Office by Biblica, Inc.™
Some scripture is taken from the New King James Version®. Copyright ©1982 by Thomas Nelson, Inc. Used by permission. All rights reserved.

The author intends no harm, and the intended purpose of this book is for emotional and spiritual encouragement. Compiled by J. Balcombe, stories written by J. Balcombe in conjunction with the people featured. Proof-read by Bev Balcombe, Marie and David Curle.

Cataloguing in Publication Data:
Title: Radical Lives Vol I
ISBN: 9-780473-386580 (pbk.)
Subjects: Biography, New Zealand Non Fiction, Christian Living
Printed and bound in New Zealand by yourbooks.co.nz
Design by wildsidedesign.net

CONTENTS

	Acknowledgements	4
	Foreword	5
1	Adrian Pritchard	7
2	Anita Mary	13
3	Bernadette Soares	19
4	Beryl Henwood	25
5	Bill Subritzky	31
6	Brian France	39
7	Cheyne Hakaraia	45
8	David Silver	53
9	Janet Balcombe	59
10	Koebi Hart	67
11	Matthew Needham	75
12	Norm McLeod	81
13	Phil Paikea	87
14	Ray Curle	93
15	Tawhiri Littlejohn	99
	Prayer	106

ACKNOWLEDGEMENTS

Thanks to the contributors featured, the ones who lived to tell the tale, for your heart and perseverance.

Thanks Matt & Nicole Danswan from Initiate Media for encouraging me to share these testimonies in Christian Life news magazine.

Thank you Ray for your love, and your hard work on *Radical Lives Vol I*, a milestone of our first year together.

Most of all, thank you Jesus.

FOREWORD

This book has been compiled from my *Christian Life* articles to inspire and encourage, not to endorse a mind-set that exploits are just for a select few.

Jesus said, *"Most assuredly, I say to you, he who believes in Me, the works that I do he will do also; and greater works than these he will do, because I go to My Father."*

It's simply a matter of surrender. Radical surrender. God does radical things in the lives of His people when they give Him everything. In these darkening days we must be ready to face anything that comes our way. There's nothing to lose and everything to gain. God is raising up His army of end-time believers. Take your place.

Janet Balcombe

Some wish to live within the sound of the chapel bell. I'd rather run a rescue mission within a yard of hell.

CT Studd

Adrian and Wendy Pritchard, and the girls

NZ edition available from
pritchardadrian@gmail.com

Australian edition available from
arkhousepress.com or **koorong.com**

ADRIAN PRITCHARD

From 'New Zealand's Most Wanted' – to life in Christ

It was like catching up with a brother from another mother, chatting with this man with Jesus shining out of his face. How did it come to be that this hardman – one of New Zealand's most notorious career criminals, came face to face with Jesus? Well, grab a coffee, put your feet up and I'll tell you. One thing is for sure; Jesus' arm is not too short to save, and His ear – not too deaf to hear.

It's a gruelling ride just reading Adrian's story *Second Chance*; never mind surviving it! Growing up, Adrian's home life was far from perfect even before his parents separated. As a teenager he didn't have a mentor to teach him the basic keys to making a living or learning a trade. He had no life skills. The stage was set for Adrian to become one of New Zealand's worst armed robbers.

A gifted teenage rugby and cricket player, his sporting career was cut short when injury struck, disillusionment crept in and drug use began at age fourteen. When Adrian was sixteen his parents separated and he was to spend the next decade and a half off-his-face on drugs and alcohol to club the pain into submission. Angry and rebellious, he lived on the streets and with friends, and relied on crime to survive. As his drug use escalated he narrowly avoided death by overdose. One day his spirit left his body and hovered over him, laughing at him. He was so wasted he couldn't even move an eyebrow, but completely dulled by the lost and hopeless state he was in at the time that the experience didn't bother him at all.

> Adrian lived on the edge and played a perpetual game of cat-and-mouse with the police and the system. He spent most of the 1990s in jails and had a cameo appearance on the police crime show, *Crime Watch*.

"In Gisborne we succeeded in ripping off just about every pharmacy, shop, bowling club and doctor's surgery. We stole something like thirty cars a year and when that wasn't enough, we did some huge hits on restaurants. We would also rob dairies and supermarkets for money and cigarettes. We carried out some of the biggest burglaries in town during our day, though it was nothing to be proud of. We would target chemists. All the drugs we stole from chemists would go straight to our personal baker to make synthetic heroin or morphine so we could shoot up. There were times when I went straight through my vein with the needle and it popped. It was painful but I just carried on with more and more drugs in my arm – a one-way ticket to death."

He left for Australia on the run from New Zealand police after attempting to burn down the Napier airport, but returned to New Zealand after eventually attracting some serious heat from Australian gangs.

After travelling to the US in pursuit of his dream of being a rock star, he returned with his dreams in shreds. Hardcore drug and sex addictions had already taken their toll and Adrian lacked the commitment to make it happen. He learned from hardened criminals and his gang associations and divided his time between Gisborne, Hastings and Auckland.

"To recap; I was now eighteen. I'd skipped the country, I'd been stabbed, involved with overseas gangs and arrested on my re-entry to New Zealand. All this, and I still hadn't dealt with my parents divorce. My major issues hadn't gotten any smaller and I still couldn't face them."

At twenty-two, doctors at Grafton Road Detox told Adrian he had the body of a seventy year old and he would be dead by twenty-five if he kept going at that rate. Eventually the system caught up with him and he landed a three-year sentence in Paremoremo Prison. Adrian began attending a prison Bible study class while still coming off heroin, cocaine and poppies. During the next two years he went cold turkey off heroin, morphine, cocaine, opium, valium and sleeping pills, to name just a few. He refused Methodone.

> "My biggest fear was going to church in jail, as it was a very different culture for me," says Adrian.

But through the prison ministry and ongoing support of Kevin and Christine Winters he saw authentic followers of Christ, and for the first time in his life, stopped running. In his prison cell one night, he invited Jesus to take over his life.

"It was the first time I felt anyone could love me! Jesus loved me the way I was and accepted me no matter what. As I lay on my bed, tears rolled down my face. Jesus was in my cell with me doing open-heart surgery. It was hard for me to transition to this new life, but it was the best decision I've ever made. Within a few weeks Jesus took away from me all desire for drugs, even while I was still going through withdrawal. He set me free. God replaced the old craving for drugs with a new-found passion for himself."

> Adrian says that being a Christian doesn't make your issues go away, but it does place a desire in your heart to put things right.

He was baptised one day on home leave. In 1998, two years after becoming a Christian and newly released from jail, Adrian had a fight with someone in the church toilets while the pastor was preaching.

"This guy was playing games with Jesus, just faking the Christian life to get what he wanted and saying false stuff about friends of mine, so I thumped him right there in the bathroom. These stubborn habits were why I needed a support system around me. I needed people I could go and talk with, like Kevin and Christine and many others."

Good friend, *Rock Priest* David Pierce of *No Longer Music* and founder of the ministry *Steiger International* (steiger.org) sponsored Adrian to do the challenging sixth-month *Lifeway Army* training in 2001 – extreme Bible college with army flavours.

Adrian has now celebrated his twelfth wedding anniversary to the beautiful Wendy and they have three gorgeous daughters. He spends his time telling people his story and showing them what Jesus looks like. He's seeking sponsorship to get his book Second Chance into prisons, to be available free for prisoners, and share the hope that we have in Christ.

"The reason I am telling my story is that I get upset and angry when I hear of young kids killing or being killed, getting into gang fights around town, or getting wasted on drugs and drink while their parents are just sitting at home. Sharing my story might help some people to break free from their lifestyle. It might even help parents talk with their children about what's going on in their lives," says Adrian.

> Salvation is found in no one else, for there is no other name under heaven given to mankind by which we must be saved.
> Acts 4:12 (NIV)

You can contact Adrian regarding sponsorship of books into prisons and rehabs, or purchase a copy on 027 659 1953, by email **pritchardadrian@gmail.com**, or visit **itt.org.nz**

Anita Mary at the Toi Ora Artists Collective
toiora.org.nz

Anita Mary, 14 years old

Anita Mary's memoir, *Blood on the Mirror*
absoluteartnz.weebly.com

ANITA MARY

Hardcore overcomer, artist and author

Our universes collided 'back in the day' in central Auckland, although we were in different scenes — Anita in hardcore punk, me in the biker crowd. You could call this a full-circle moment. Anita has been in dark places but was always one of God's kids behind enemy lines. Growing up in Shirley, Christchurch in the late 1960's, Anita's only constant was change. After a tumultuous first four years of life the fighting finally stopped when Anita's Dad left for good.

As a youngster she went to an after-school Christian group called *The Sunshine Club* run by Ray Comfort and his wife. Anita learned about a guy called Jesus and that he was some kind of 'bridge' thing — she didn't know what would happen if she gave her heart to Him, but she did, and everyone clapped. She never understood why. When she went home, life continued as before.

A nightmare of childhood sexual abuse and eighteen schools later, Anita ran away from home at age fifteen to be 'free.' What she found, however, was everything but freedom. On the streets of Auckland and Wellington a classic tragedy played out; of self-hatred, suicide attempts, abortions, clinical depression and many other mental illness diagnoses, drug-addiction, promiscuity and prostitution. Through it all she expressed herself by writing and drawing her thoughts, dreams and visions. In the late 1980s Anita immersed herself in the New Plymouth Hardcore Scene. Her nickname *Looney On A Wheel* encapsulated her non-stop craving for affection, attention and addictive substances.

In 1990 an accident left her encased in the car. By the time they had her cut out she had been deceased for six to eight minutes. With severe brain injuries, temporary paralysis on one side and a stroke on the other, she was in a coma for fifteen days. Against all odds Anita learned to walk, talk and write all over again. In spite of a deep resentment towards God for allowing certain things to happen to her, His hand on her life was evident.

In her search for belonging and purpose it wasn't long before Anita's world closed in on her again. After several drug treatment programmes she found herself pregnant once more. Her miracle son was born. Alone, with deep dissatisfaction in her heart, she spiraled down again and was put on Methadone and other prescription meds. In 2000 she met David. He kept mentioning this Jesus guy.

> "When He started talking about Jesus, it felt like warm liquid was being poured over me and into my heart."

She went to church with David and gave her life to Jesus Christ after being *'kicked out of the chair by something'* when the altar-call was made. She was baptised, came off Methadone and other drugs and found the hole in her heart was finally filled. In 2001 Anita met Brad, they married in 2002 and a whole new exciting chapter began.

Anita still struggles with pain as a result of the accident and joined the Auckland Regional Pain Service (ARPS). She uses art to document her journey through hell to wholeness and beyond. Art therapist Janet McLeod saw Anita's talent and took her to the Toi Ora Artists Collective in 2011 where she is a current board member. She exhibits her paintings and is involved in the local community in Papakura, where she lives with her husband and son. They attend Life South in Auckland.

Anita released her first book, her autobiography, *Blood On The Mirror* in October 2016 at Toi Ora Studio. It tells her story from the streets, overcoming mental illness and addiction, to freedom in Christ includes art to illustrate the chapters of her life. Anita captures images on canvas that inspire others to see their value. Today, because of her relationship with Jesus and the restoration in her life, Anita is a bridge for those who've gone where she has been.

> "LOVE was the most difficult choice for me to make. But once I had exhausted all other options, my hurt becomes HOPE."

Anita is used to being misunderstood. As a child, things just used to go wrong when she wanted them to go right. As an adult and a heavily tattooed Christian woman she is no stranger to whispers and judgment. But Anita doesn't judge those who judge her, but chooses to bless them.

Anita is no longer a *Looney On A Wheel*, but a princess of the King and a *Life Of Absolute Wonder* for such a time as this.

> "My life is no longer my own. The life I have lived allows me to empathise with those battling injustice, lies and searching for meaning."

Anita Mary is on **AbsoluteArtnz.com** and on Facebook.

"When I passed by you again and looked upon you, indeed your time was the time of love; so I spread My wing over you and covered your nakedness. Yes, I swore an oath to you and entered into a covenant with you, and you became Mine," says the Lord God.

"Then I washed you in water; yes, I thoroughly washed off your blood, and I anointed you with oil."

Ezekiel 16:8-9 (NKJV)

'Emerging'

*Crossing The Bloodline
– lessons learnt on my knees*

Anita Mary is working on her second book which is due for release 2018

Top:
Bernadette Soares

Middle:
The Soares family (from left), Reuben, Clyde, Bernadette, Gideon and Gaby

Left:
Bernadette on the podium, first in 100m sprint

BERNADETTE SOARES

On wings like eagles

We met at a conference where Bernadette was doing what she does in her 'spare' time – encouraging and empowering others to soar. Bernadette owns four Australasian women's beauty brands, has a great faith, and a stunning family.

Once you get past the striking beauty, you can't help notice the unapologetic success of this serial entrepreneur and think, *"It's probably always been easy for her."* But we would be very wrong.

> "God knew what my challenges in life would be and He needed to ground me in faith, perseverance, fortitude and grace," says Bernadette.

She was a natural over-achiever and sports-woman at a national level (she hates me saying that). Growing up in Bombay, India, the traditional religion in which she grew up had weekly confession. At seven or eight years old Bernadette had to borrow sins from sisters and brothers just to look like a repentant sinner.

As a teenager she knew that something was missing and there had to be more to faith in God. Yearning for excitement, her entrepreneurial spirit was taking flight and she needed this to translate to her faith. At fifteen, Bernadette met a group of missionaries at college and began attending Bible classes. When they shared the gospel and asked if she wanted to accept this living, active and alive faith in Jesus, she couldn't get born-again quickly enough!

> Bernadette rushed home to share the good news with her supportive family only to find they were horrified to hear of her new faith in Jesus. She was forbidden to see her new friends and told she could pack up and leave home if she didn't obey.

There was no social welfare system in India at that time. The missionaries told Bernadette she was welcome to go back to America with them. Her heart was in terrible turmoil. She didn't know that God directs and speaks to us personally until she heard God clearly say she should stay home and respect her parents, and that what God had put in her heart would never be taken away from her.

Bernadette was forbidden to share her faith and it was kept as a shameful family secret. Thus began three long years of isolation from other believers, but she read her Bible and trusted God to fill her, lead and guide her, which He did. God gave her strength to face the family who believed she had been brainwashed, but they could see her determination to live out her faith. Her mother cried for her and Bernadette was told that if her father's pre-existing heart condition caused any problems it would be her fault.

Bernadette recognises this intense time as a baby Christian leaning on God alone as her training ground for life, and particularly business. It strengthened her to keep believing when others didn't see the vision or end result. At age eighteen, Bernadette met her future husband, Clyde, who became a Christian shortly after they met. Clyde and Bernadette moved to New Zealand and now have three passionate and talented kids, Gideon, Gaby and Reuben.

As a little girl Bernadette always knew she was called to business and was reared on stories of her entrepreneurial grandmother who was tough, honest and fair. However, after a few years in business, things got tough. She was a wife and mother to two teenagers and one pre-teen and had been challenged a few times by other women (mostly) if God had really called her into business. To this point she had just followed her heart and natural abilities.

> Feeling a little jaded, Bernadette took a week's retreat to really seek God for direction. To continue on in business, or to walk away?

Pastors Graham and Shona were at Titoki House at that time. Bernadette hadn't told anyone what she was seeking God for, but in her very first session God told Shona to *"anoint her for business."* God is no time-waster and got down to business straight away, leaving the remaining five days for Bernadette to be enriched, invigorated and spiritually grounded, with her feet firmly in the business arena.

From one product and one brand, God did amazing things, multiplying what Bernadette gave Him. She had started in 2002 with a recipe from her mother-in-law for a hair removal product that she cooked on her stove-top and sold from her door. Today her four beauty brands have over one hundred products under the *Brand Value* umbrella **brandvalue.co.nz**. Core business is selling directly to spas and salons. God has taken Bernadette's humble beginnings and developed some award-winning products that have succeeded beyond all expectations.

> God doesn't give your calling and talents to make you more important, richer or better than others. He gives us talents to use for His glory and kingdom," says Bernadette.

After a speaking engagement in Kawerau, Bernadette set up the charity *Let Your Light Shine*, whose vision is to empower individuals to realise their God-given dreams. She is putting her Economics and Commerce background to good effect and learning how small towns can grow to be economical and financial hubs using their natural resources.

Bernadette means business. In less than a year, God has helped to open doors in Kawerau that only He could open and she is actively working with the other Churches, KEA (Kawerau Economic Agency) and the Kawerau District Council towards the economic wellbeing of the region.

Clyde, a successful businessman in his own right, also finds time to work with the High School kids in Kawerau teaching them Maths and Science.

The vision for *Let Your Light Shine* is to become a model for economic, financial and spiritual growth for other small towns across New Zealand, many of which have been abandoned by big business and central government... but not forgotten by God.

The website **shine-nz.org** has more information on their work in the Kawerau region to identify viable ideas and grow them into tangible businesses. You can contact Bernadette via the website if you would like to get involved, or to invite her to speak in your community.

From everyone who has been given much, much will be demanded; and from the one who has been entrusted with much, much more will be asked.
Luke 12:48 (NIV)

Top: Beryl and grandson Brent *Middle:* Ken and Beryl *Bottom:* Bill's last summer
Battle Cry is available from **henwood@maxnet.co.nz**

BERYL HENWOOD

The warrior woman who emerged from the crucible of personal tragedy shining as gold

Beryl doesn't look like your stereotypical warrior, but is unquestionably an asset in stealth mode. Her intestinal fortitude is exceptional. I like that. Her life exhibits character I can only pray I would possess in the same trials, but this can never truly be known until the rubber meets the road.

The family moved around a lot while she was growing up after her parents' divorce. Life was difficult and Beryl was well acquainted with lack as the family struggled to make ends meet. Being part Rotuman Islander, she walked closely with rejection and resentment caused by racial intolerance. She believed she was ugly, stupid and unpopular so when the dashing, sophisticated pilot Ken came into her life when she was seventeen, it wasn't long before Beryl was pregnant. She was pressured to adopt. Her doctor prescribed her Valium to cope with the grief, and a ten-year habit began.

Ken and Beryl married and an extremely tumultuous few years ensued. They had two girls, Ken worked seven days a week and was hardly home. Unable to cope, Beryl had an abortion which was followed by deep depression, self-hatred, overwhelming grief — and much more Valium. Ken suffered terrible headaches and black moods, and they both longed to be free of the misery they inflicted on each other. Beryl left for the second time, taking the girls with her.

She began to pray the Lord's prayer with desperation and to really think about what it meant. Outwardly life was all parties, restaurants, and entertainment but inwardly it was a nightmare of fear and confusion. Her life was out of control and she felt powerless to break the pattern.

Lonely and desperate, one evening Ken picked up a Bible and began to read. He read all four Gospels that day and suddenly he knew it was true. He believed for the first time. On his knees, Ken repented before God. He felt something leave him and then a great peace came upon him. From that moment he changed, and then moved to be closer to Beryl and the girls.

But Beryl still had no peace and by now had added Mogadon to her prescription drug-fest. Desperate, she cried out, "God if you're real; tell me what to do!" Then, filling the room came an authoritative, gentle male voice, *"Go back to Ken."*

Classic. So she did, although she was still hard-hearted and unhappy. Ken was kind but then seemed to put his faith aside, and they both explored alternate avenues of finding peace, but were still resistant to church.

Nevertheless after a co-worker had prayed and fasted for Beryl for months, Beryl became willing to attend a church meeting held at a pub. Touched by the Holy Spirit, she saw all her sin and pain, and felt a great surge of love pouring through her in a classic salvation experience. For the first time in her life she felt truly loved, accepted and whole. She was baptised and began to pray that Ken would come to the Lord in a deep and committed way.

One freaky thing about life is that we just never know when we're saying goodbye to someone for the last time. Ken gradually softened to the things of God over the next three years, but he wasn't to fully surrender his life and be filled with the Holy Spirit until seven days before his death. But those seven days were heaven.

> After receiving the call that her husband's plane had gone down in severe conditions, Beryl ignored her emotions and out of faith prayed the most amazing thanksgiving prayer, praising Jesus for what He had done in their lives. Indestructible peace descended on Beryl and the house.

Although everyone was praying for Ken's survival, Beryl knew he'd gone. So deep was Beryl's peace that she was able to comfort the grieving visitors in their loss; even through Ken's memorial service three weeks later.

> Many gave their lives to Christ because of the peace and strength Beryl carried through that terrible time with God's incredible grace.

Beryl poured herself into serving the Lord, and after a few years, she met Bill and remarried. Along with Bill's young son and Beryl's two daughters, God blessed them with a boy and girl, making a beautiful new family. Over the years Beryl had attempted to find her adopted son but to no avail.

Then one day, after having been obedient to a prompt from the Lord to make another call to find him, Beryl received a phone call. *"Hello Mum."* Her son had a wife and a baby boy. *"You say you're a Christian. What sort of Christian are you?"* he asked. *"I'm a spirit-filled, tongue-speaking Christian,"* Beryl answered. He laughed and said, *"So am I."* God had told the social welfare officer organising his placement, **"This baby must go to a Christian home."**

Beryl and Bill have fostered teenagers, trained at the *Youth with a Mission* (YWAM) Discipleship Training School (DTS), worked in Hong Kong for Jackie Pullinger helping minister to heroin addicts, and smuggled Bibles into China three times.

God showed Beryl His broken heart over abortion and she helped save dozens of babies outside an abortion clinic by offering hope and support to desperate mothers. She wrote for the *Pro Life Times* and speaks and counsels on this issue. Bill and Beryl were involved with *YWAM* since 1990.

The Lord taught Beryl how to warfare in the spirit for individuals, homes, businesses, churches, communities and nations. She saw God sovereignly restore the area and people of Gate Pa in Tauranga through her team working alongside local Maori during a week of spiritual warfare. On the last night they prayed for the grandson of the Chief. The Chief had been a godly man who had recently died, and the grandson took up his mantle. Beryl and the team saw a breakthrough with the Tuhoi people in the Urewera Ranges after much spiritual warfare and a sovereign move of God.

> Beryl has ministered to witches leaving covens; and seen chronic illness, depression and demonic oppression healed in Jesus name.

Then Jesus visited her and asked her to make another tough journey. That tough journey was saying goodbye to Bill as the Lord took him home after a battle with cancer. Sometimes God has to take the big Kauri trees to make way for the young ones. Bill had run his race well, and once again, it was just Beryl and her God. And once again she has come through shining as gold through the toughest of trials. Beryl now heads up *YWAM Zion* in Paparoa, Northland.

It's criminal how many epic parts of Beryl's story I have had to leave out in this short article. She is an inspiration and a generous gift to our generation. Seriously, you need to get her book! For your copy of *Battle Cry,* email her on **henwood@maxnet.co.nz** or buy it on Kindle from Amazon.com (still under the original title, *The Oil of Joy for Mourning*).

Top:
Bill and Kaylene Subritzky

Bottom:
Bill speaking at the Faith Revival Conference in Tawau, Sabah, Malaysia

BILL SUBRITZKY

Where angels fear to tread

It's hard to live in New Zealand and not to have at least heard about our most well-known evangelist, Bill Subritzky. I'd never been to one of his healing meetings but enjoyed his video teachings *Receiving the Gifts of the Holy Spirit* and *Deliverance from Demons* series. I also enjoyed my husband Ray's many stories of working the prayer and deliverance lines with Bill. Especially memorable was when a demon who Bill had obviously evicted from someone else before, addressed him by saying, *"So, we meet again, Preacher!"*

It was a blast to meet Bill face to face at his 90th birthday celebration where he was honoured by several senior pastors for the decades he has faithfully preached the Gospel of Jesus Christ. Apostle Viliamu (founder and head of one hundred Samoan churches worldwide) shared how his nation has changed since Bill preached the gospel and ministered in God's power to them.

But this successful lawyer and businessman came from the most humble of beginnings and used to collect and sell firewood during the depression to help the family survive. Then, when he was eight years old, Bill's younger brother contracted cancer at five years old, and died at home after nine agonising months. Years later his mother told Bill that on the day Keith died they heard him calling from his bedroom, *"Mummy and Daddy, come here quickly!"*

> To their amazement, Keith was sitting up on the bed looking perfectly well. He wasn't looking at them but looking upwards with great expectation, and he said, *"Mummy and Daddy, I've got to go now."* The angels of God had come for him.

As a result of their son's death, Bill's parents began searching for God. They had been nominal Christians and ended up in a very closed Brethren group. Bill attended that church for some years but when he was sixteen he told his parents he no longer wanted to attend church. It was very legalistic and he felt too confined. He wasn't allowed to listen to the radio, go to movies or sports. However his mother often quoted the Word of God to him and he still remembers many of those Scriptures.

Determined to become a lawyer, Bill qualified and at age twenty-one started his own law practice. Then he met and married Pat. She was a practising Anglican but Bill was not committed to God and had only joined the church to make business contacts. However, God had other plans.

One day Bill's teenage daughter Maria became a committed Christian and he went with her to a meeting. He watched the preacher pray for one of his clients. She was elderly and could barely walk because she was full of arthritis. As the lady was being prayed for, she fell to the floor and Bill thought she'd died, but she jumped up and shouted she was healed. That got his attention! He was astounded and excited by the power of God.

Although his marriage had gradually got into difficulties, he and Pat and their children attended a crusade in Hamilton conducted by the same preacher. They went again the next night and again he felt the desire to surrender his life to Christ. This desire became overpowering, and finally he raised his hand at the altar-call, along with Pat and the whole family.

The preacher told all those who had raised their hands to come to the front. When he knelt down and confessed his sins, Bill did his best and prayed the sinner's prayer although he didn't feel anything special happen at the time. The preacher offered the experience of being "baptised into the Holy Spirit." Bill didn't know what he was talking about but Maria pressed him to go forward for this baptism, to his amazement when the preacher laid hands on him Bill spoke in tongues. Bill went back to Auckland almost in a daze.

"The next morning when I looked out of my bedroom window I had never seen the grass so green, the trees so beautiful or heard the birds sing like that before. I looked at the sky and I had never seen it so blue. I realised that I was looking at the earth with new eyes, that I was born-again."

Then Bill made one of the most important decisions of his life. He resolved to turn 180° from darkness to light, from the power of Satan, to the power of God.

"This has saved me from many difficulties and problems, and since then I have always known the presence and power of God within me at all times."

He witnessed to his legal partners in due course, and they became born-again Christians too. His marriage was immediately healed and for the next forty years he ministered together with Pat in the power and love of the Holy Spirit.

Within a week of their commitment to Christ they started a prayer meeting in their home, and many people were saved, healed and delivered over the following eight years.

It was in those meetings that for the first time in his life Bill saw demonic powers manifest in people and he learned how to cast them out in Jesus name. He learned to minister in the gifts of the Holy Spirit including the word of wisdom, word of knowledge, faith, healings, working of miracles, discerning of spirits as in 1 Corinthians 12.

Bill was soon invited to speak at various churches and conferences around New Zealand, then overseas where he spoke at seven world conventions of the Full Gospel Businessmen's

Fellowship in various countries including the USA, the Philippines and Brazil.

He conducted crusades around the Pacific including Hawaii, Fiji, the Solomon Islands, Samoa, Vanuatu, Tonga and throughout Australia where literally tens of thousands responded to the Gospel of Jesus Christ and received physical healing.

"I promised the Lord that I would preach the Gospel in every town in New Zealand, over the years I have done so from Te Hapua in the uppermost part of the North Island, right throughout the South Island including the Chatham Islands, as well as Great Barrier Island."

> "I have also been privileged to preach the Gospel in various places in Africa, Canada, England, Mexico, the USA and South America. Also throughout Asia including India, Japan, Malaysia and Singapore. Again, it has been a privilege to see untold numbers come forward and give their lives to Christ and receive mighty healings and deliverances."

Bill always preached on the basis of what Jesus said: *"Repent and believe the Gospel."* He believes the primary work of the Holy Spirit is to convict of sin, righteousness and judgment. Accordingly he has preached the need for absolute repentance from sin, as well as the grace of God and walking in true holiness.

For approximately ten years *Youth for Christ* conducted an annual camp for young people on Bill's farm near Kerikeri. Bill spoke there and through God's grace saw thousands of young people commit their lives to Christ. His two sons Paul and John lead the ministry of *Promise Keepers* in New Zealand where for the past twenty-one years, thousands of men have come to Christ and many have seen their marriages restored.

Four years ago, after many years of happy marriage and walking with the Lord, Bill's wife Pat passed into glory. Then in a miraculous set of circumstances the Lord led Bill and Kaylene into marriage a year later. "Kaylene is absolutely committed to the Lord and works strongly in prophecy and the word of knowledge. She is a very able preacher. We have a wonderful marriage."

Over the years Bill has prayed on radio for many to be healed and come to Christ. There have been many great testimonies of Christ's healing power from these broadcasts as well as the teaching series on radio. Recently the Holy Spirit spoke to Bill about praying for the sick on Skype and he began a powerful monthly webcast programme.

> "Luke 6:17 says that Jesus often healed people at a distance and we can see this today when we pray for the sick at a distance. "As my wife Kaylene and I pray on Skype we see the power of God touch people in an amazing way."

"They may be living in the USA or Australia or Dubai but the same Holy Spirit touches them all. We stand amazed as we see the fire of God passing through people and healing them on Skype and at the reports from others watching who are being touched."

In 1991 Bill was awarded the Queen Service Medal for his services to the community. He passed away in December 2015.

Before he established Dove Ministries, Bill was a senior partner in a large law firm in Auckland for 33 years, and also the founder and Governing Director of one of New Zealand's largest home building companies, Universal Homes. He travelled and ministered throughout New Zealand, Australia, the South Pacific, Indonesia, Singapore and Malaysia, as well as the USA, South America, England and Europe and parts of Africa.

Bill's 14 books and other resources are available either free or at a low cost at **doveministries.com** including the bestseller, 'Demons Defeated'.

Amazing Grace, how sweet the sound,
That saved a wretch like me.
I once was lost but now I'm found,
Was blind, but now I see.

Top:
Brian France, *Promise Keepers NZ* promo

Middle:
The site of the blast in Londonderry,
Northern Ireland

Left:
Brian today

BRIAN FRANCE

An Irish bombshell with the power of God

Now it's not every day you meet a guy who was blown up by an IRA bomb... and lived to tell the tale. And yet there he is, larger than life, standing in front of me conducting my brother-in-law's wedding with not a hair out of place.

Brian was an officer in the Royal Air Force Regiment serving as a Platoon Commander in Northern Ireland as part of the British security forces. This was in the early 1970s during the time of the 'Troubles' when the Irish Republican Army (IRA) was endeavouring by the force of terrorism to have the six Northern Counties reunited with the rest of Ireland. Two-thirds of the population didn't want reunification so the terrorism with its bombings, snipers, petrol bombs, sectarian murders, kneecappings and bloodshed continued.

The Royal Air Force Regiment had been deployed in Northern Ireland as part of the peacekeeping forces for some years and this was Brian's third tour of duty. He was now responsible for the security of the Walled City of Londonderry. It was early March, the weather was cold and damp, and his men were on the streets providing both mobile and standing patrols. As unexploded bombs were discovered, his men cordoned off the area and called the Bomb Disposal Squad. In dealing with the aftermath of bomb explosions they did what they could for the injured, and kept people from entering damaged buildings. Five bombs had already gone off when Brian was alerted to bomb number six, an unexploded bomb, by a radio message from the Control Centre.

> "It took a second or two for me to realise that the shop I was standing in had a bomb planted there ready to explode. I turned to my left and was going to shout, "Get out!" to my senior sergeant who was coming in behind me. I never quite got those words out as at that instant an estimated fifteen pounds of high explosive went off a metre behind me."

In a flash, his entire world was dominated by the exploding bomb as the sound of it momentarily became his whole existence. The detonation completely demolished the room, stripping the linings off the walls, bringing down the ceiling and blasting a large hole in the floor. It picked Brian up in its destructive grip, doing it's best to destroy him as he was hurled out the front of the bakery, along with a mass of debris.

"The force of the blast threw me about eight metres, and I found myself lying on the road at the front of the shop, with bricks, smashed wooden beams and a mass of rubble around and over me."

Fortunately Brian was wearing a flak jacket made up of laminated layers of fibreglass with a green nylon cover. The jacket's function was to protect his vital organs from the flak produced by bomb explosions. And that's exactly what it did.

> The end result of being blown up was that he was invalided out of the RAF with no hearing, and legs that didn't work properly because they were full of shrapnel.

Walking was excruciating with hundreds of tiny pieces of metal in his muscles, knees and ankle joints. The larger pieces of metal had been removed by surgeons who had also stitched together a large wound in the back of his head.

His hearing was so badly damaged, it may as well have been non-existent. When he asked to have hearing-aids he was told, "Sorry fella, you don't have enough hearing to amplify; they'll do you no good. So get used to being profoundly deaf. That's how you're going to spend the rest of your life."

Brian came to New Zealand and for three years, lip-read and guessed his way through conversations with "umm," "well I never!" and, "is that so?" being his major contributions. He refused a wheelchair and did all he could do to get his legs functioning again.

One sunny day out while shopping in Darfield, near Christchurch, he bumped into a small group of Christian street evangelists who, on discovering he was deaf, asked if they could pray for his hearing. Brian was brought up with the understanding that "seeing is believing," so he figured that as he couldn't hear now, they couldn't do him any harm. He let them give it a go.

He went with them to a nearby house where they sat him in a chair and prayed for his hearing to be restored. Absolutely nothing happened. Brian went to bed that night as deaf as he had ever been.

> "However, in the morning I was awakened by the ticking of a small electric clock that sat on my bedside table. I leapt out of bed with incredible relief, realising that I could hear and the deafness nightmare was over."

This was a life-transforming event. Overnight, God's healing power had restored the damage the explosion had caused, and it changed Brian's life. He went from being largely unemployable, depressed, non-productive and feeling useless, to suddenly having the potential of a full life again – apart from his legs, which only functioned with considerable pain.

About a week later, Brian was shopping in Darfield again and bumped into the same group of Christians. He told them of his healing and thanked them profusely for praying for him. They jumped around shouting "Hallelujah!" and "Praise the Lord!" They chatted for a few minutes and were about to part when he had a sudden thought.

"They had prayed for my hearing and it had been restored; what if they were to pray for the pain in my legs?" Brian thought.

The group enthusiastically agreed to do this and took him to the same house, into the same room and sat him in the same chair. Placing their hands upon his legs they asked the Lord Jesus to remove the pain. As they prayed, Brian felt the pain drain down his legs and out of his feet. He has had no pain in his legs since!

God really got his attention that day, and Brian realised that the "seeing is believing" worldview on which he had been brought up, was false. He now understands that what the Bible says is true, that "believing is seeing."

> "If we want to minister in miracles, we must first accept that God is a supernatural God of miracles, just like the Bible says."

Brian now leads a team at *Charisma Christian Ministries* and facilitates a weekly healing meeting every week in Auckland. His team often travelled with and supported the international healing meetings conducted by evangelist Bill Subritzky. Check out **charisma.org.nz**

"Not by might nor by power, but by my Spirit," says the Lord of hosts.
Zachariah 4:6 (NKJV)

Top: Cheyne's *Move the Crowd* promo pic
Left: Cheyne heavily addicted to Meth and patched up with the Mangu Kaha
Right: Cheyne and Analisa

CHEYNE HAKARAIA

True pedigree

As soon as my husband Ray and I saw him while on our honeymoon at Treetops Lodge in the mountains near Rotorua, I knew there was something special about him. It was more than his genuine servant heart, humility and spirit of excellence. The Holy Spirit was all over Cheyne. There was no clue of the sexual abuse, depression and suicidal tendencies he had survived, or the gangster of days gone by.

Cheyne bears a striking resemblance to his Grandfather, Frederick Augustus Bennett, who was the world's First Maori Anglican Bishop at St Faith's, Ohinemutu. His ancestral pedigree hails from the Te Arawa Tribe and the Ngati Whakaue chiefly line and includes grand uncle Sir Charles Bennett who was the second Maori to go to Oxford University, a highly decorated soldier, High Commissioner to the Federation of Malaya in the early 1960s and a Labour Party President in the 1970s. Cheyne's other grand uncle, Dr Henry Bennett, was a respected leader in the field of Maori mental health and was also a highly decorated soldier.

Rich heritage also flows from the Hakaraia line. Cheyne is a mokopuna (grandchild) of Sonny Hakaraia who was the President of the K-force returned soldiers, and also master carver/kapa haka founder of Nagti Whakaue Te Arawa waka, Kima Hakaraia.

Of Samoan-Maori descent, Cheyne is the oldest of five boys brought up in Koutu, Rotorua by his mother and stepfather. His father left before Cheyne was born. But sexual abuse marred his childhood and led to promiscuity. At school he was already playing gangster, selling and growing weed. His stepfather was in and out of jail and his mother finally cried out to Jesus and was born again. God's goodness touched Cheyne's heart through the Monday night family dinners at Lake City Church (pre-Destiny) run by Waru and Elaine Herbert, where he gained a foundation in the things of God.

After leaving school Cheyne worked at a mill while rapping and DJ'ing evenings and writing music. The drug use got heavier and now included hallucinogenics and his journey into the gang lifestyle began with the Crips. Cheyne's uncle and street-father was a very well respected man and like the Godfather in Rotorua and he had the power to de-patch anyone from any gang and a founding member of the Filthy Few in NZ. Cheyne founded the OKB's – *Original Koutu Bruthers* (whom he tries to help today) and ran lucrative tinny shops.

Cheyne brought LSD and speed into the hood, moving quickly from low-quality speed to being amongst the first to smoke pure Meth. He learned how to cook and saw Meth spread like a plague across NZ.

He was making a lot of money and running his own crews when Cheyne decided to step back and do some music promoting. He got into the hip hop scene in Auckland, did a few gigs with Short Khop who rolled with Ice Cube. He busted some rhymes with King Kapisi and hung out with Ché-Fu and many other artists. Cheyne brought US hip hop acts Krayzie Bone and Bone Thugs & Harmony, and Coolio from Gangstas Paradise down to Rotorua for sold-out shows.

The event was a success on the ground in spite of an onslaught of ugly challenges including the deal going bad with the corrupt US promoter, sabotage by Mai FM and the ensuing legal battle. However, already in heavy addiction the stress left Cheyne burnt-out and depressed and he called out to God in desperation, but this connection with God was to be short-lived.

After hanging out with the King Cobras he got fully patched up with the MKs (Mangu Kaha).

> Now heavily involved in the meth trade, Cheyne became known as *The Pedigree Man* because of the unequalled quality of his gear. His crew were the moneymakers.

Smoking a gram a session, 20 grams a week and staying awake for up to two weeks at a time, things never were going to end well. Kidnappings and robberies were business as usual.

Cheyne's entrepreneurial talent served him well on the dark side. He was very good at being very bad. He began importing the raw material for meth (pseudoephedrine) after infiltrating the

Asian-backed tourism players in Rotorua. His Asian crew imported premium quality gear masked as health products. Cheyne's pure product caused problems in the hood with rival players and even his own president got jealous. Paranoid and psychotic he could hear choppers all the time and thought the gang was going to whack him. He armed himself for war with the biggest gun heist in Rotorua but sold the guns and made more cash. Money was his God.

Rock bottom in New Zealand was fast approaching. In deep depression and two suicide attempts later, Cheyne's girlfriend left him for his mate. He'd had enough of his gang and the feeling was mutual, so he got out.

Making a new start in Sydney, Australia, Cheyne started a removals business. He thought he'd seen all he ever wanted to see of hell, but his cousins were top-level gangsters in Australia and the odds were against him. He fell hard for Ecstasy and the vicious cycle repeated — using, dealing, then cooking E.

> The Darling Harbour gangster boat party scene was his first top-dog encounter with Mafia from every country represented; supermodels, gang heads, cocaine, glamour and money everywhere. His cousin was head of one of the biggest bike gangs in Australia with connections to South American cartels.

Cheyne descended to new depths. Delusions of grandeur gave way to perverse fantasies and once again Cheyne's body and mind began to cave under the strain, so he returned to New Zealand.

Back in Rotorua, Cheyne tried once again to make a new start and completed a Diploma of Tourism at Sir George Seymour College. He went back to church but was still smoking dope.

> God told Cheyne if he didn't change his ways he was going to die or go to jail for a very long time, and he knew God's grace had run out.

Then he met his wife-to-be, the beautiful Analisa. The biggest irony of all — she was a cop! On their first date he fell hard for her and spilled the whole truth about his past. It was to be a rough ride. The clash of the kingdoms was always going to be interesting and hanging out with cops was not Cheyne's forte. Cheyne assaulted a cop over a very minor dispute and his bail conditions involved not seeing Ana. She was reprimanded and endured disciplinary procedures. The force did everything in their power to break them up and use her against him in court.

The Lord delivered them but relationship problems continued, and Cheyne went back on meth and cocaine. Ana left him and met another guy.

Cheyne heard the Lord say, *"Keep chasing her, fight for her and she will be the one."*

He asked her what she liked about the other guy and although

Ana was not saved, she said,

"*He's a man of God. After everything I've been through I've now found what I wanted. A kingdom man.*"

At this, Cheyne recommitted his life to God properly and knew this would be the real deal. His journey of true repentance and forgiveness began and he set about becoming the best husband and father he could be.

He confessed the childhood abuse and received prayer and healing. Ana's daughter Jorlena gave her life to Christ then led Ana to the Lord. Cheyne's Samoan father attended the wedding and it was a time of special restoration. Ana and Cheyne are drug and alcohol-free, spirit-filled, they pray and fast together and head up a cell-group.

The Destiny Church initiative *Man Up* empowers men to discover purpose and maximise potential and take ownership of their lives. Cheyne now runs *Man Up* in Koutu, one of many running throughout the country. Ana leads the charge with the women in the church, and new ones around her. She participates in regular prayer sessions at the Rotorua police station.

Cheyne and Ana honour their spiritual father, Bishop Brian Tamaki, and spiritual mother Hannah Tamaki, and local pastors Rewi and Davina Hare, for being role models of incredible Godly influence in their lives, and for how they encourage Maori men to rise up.

Cheyne's ministry is all about kingdom living and healing. The vision of reaching people for Jesus with his *Move the Crowd* 2015 tour came while he was still in the gangs.

> Today Cheyne's true pedigree comes from the one true King, Jesus Christ, and he needs no other.

Cheyne now runs his own entertainment business with DJ's and sound rigs, and a building business (Buildflex Solutions). Ana has since left the police and now works with Cheyne. There is a book in the pipeline.

You can find **Cheyne Hakaraia** on Facebook, *buildflexsolutions* and *RulenReign*.

But seek first the kingdom of God and His righteousness, and all these things shall be added to you.
Matthew 6:33 (NKJV)

Top:
David & Josie Silver in Israel

Right:
A Slow Train Coming

— *God's redemption plan for Israel and the Church*

DAVID SILVER

The reluctant Messianic Jew evangelist

David Silver is a Messianic Jew. He's a friend I haven't met yet, but my husband Ray speaks of him often and they keep in touch. He attended a home-group with Ray many years ago, and now ministers all around the world.

He was born in Auckland in 1955 to Jewish parents. His parents weren't devout. They attended synagogue on the Holy days and on the odd occasion. David went to Sabbath School most Saturdays. He recalls enjoying being Jewish when he was young, but rejected his Jewish roots and rebelled against his parents after his Bar-Mitzvah.

At high school David became best friends with Barry Curle, a brother of my husband, the son of a well-known New Zealand evangelist, George Curle. He kept the fact that he used to hang around the local church a secret from his parents.

"Even though we only went to the church to meet girls and keep my friend's parents happy, I can remember that we were the prime targets of the church 'Bible-bashers.' I can recall being really challenged and having a strange feeling inside," David says.

However, at that time all he was interested in was having a good time, and for the next seventeen years David lived his life according to his own ideals. He totally rejected the existence of God and had his own philosophies about life. He believed in evolution and UFOs, and was dedicated to divorcing himself from anything Jewish.

David believed Christianity was just a crutch for people who were at rock bottom; alcoholics, drug addicts, people with broken marriages and the like. David's life was just the opposite – he was living the kiwi dream. Happily married, he had a two-year old son and another on the way, a partner in a successful business, a brand new house and a BMW. He spent his spare time windsurfing, skiing and generally enjoying life, and a nightly joint and a few beers solved any problems or stresses that came along.

> One day, David's wife, Josie, dropped a bombshell. She had become a born-again Christian. David felt very threatened by this and feared it would mean the end of their marriage, or at the very least, a severe cramping of his lifestyle.

It's funny how when we hear someone else's good news our first reaction is often, "But wait, how does that affect me?" David was angry, and for six months did everything he could to convince her she'd been brainwashed, and to give it up. He then changed tack and tried to prove that Christianity was a farce and it was only the power of her own mind that had brought about these radical changes in her life. Poor Josie!

Then his friend Barry got saved, and the next week gave David a video called *Rock and Roll Seminar – A Search For God*. He was really into music and this video blew him away. Here were many of the artists and bands that he loved and they were promoting occult and satanic behavior. Almost without exception they blasphemed the name of Jesus. The album covers had an unreasonable number of bizarre depictions of the cross and many had pictures of Satan and demons. He was shocked, and immediately convinced of the reality of the devil and his evil works and concluded that if Satan was real, then God must be as well. He believed.

David knew what he had to do, but it took twenty-four hours for him to finally pray and ask for God's forgiveness and to invite Jesus to be his Lord and Savior. He asked for a sign to help strengthen his new faith.

> "The next Sunday at church, I had a real supernatural experience as I felt something come right into the centre of my being. It was hot and as it went back out of me, it seemed to take away the hardness and wickedness of my heart. I was prayed for at the end of the service and again the Spirit of God came upon me in a mighty way. I was convinced."

David's faith grew stronger week by week and he was baptised in water and by the Holy Spirit. At first he believed he could totally deny being Jewish and tell people that he was a Christian.

After a few months, the Lord sent people to him who spoke about their friends who were Jewish believers three times in as many days.

> God opened his eyes to the reality of how precious it was to be one of God's chosen people, and to be a believer in the Messiah. He soon understood that God had chosen him for a special purpose, and he believes that purpose is to help other Jewish people and others to find Jesus as their personal Messiah.

David told Josie that he believed the Lord was directing them to immigrate to Israel. She was definitely not in agreement, so he prayed and suggested that if God wanted their family in Israel He needed to show Josie personally. A few days later Josie had a vision and a song and she immediately knew what the meaning was. So they began the process of Aliyah (the immigration of Jews back to Israel) and six months later, having sold everything, were in Haifa, Israel. They have been living on Mount Carmel ever since.

David runs *Out of Zion Ministries*, has ministered in forty countries over the last fifteen years and featured on Shine TV's *In Focus* programme.

Josie runs an Internet-based intercession ministry for Israel.

David's book, *A Slow Train Coming*, which outlines God's redemptive plan for Israel, is available on **out-of-zion.com** in Chinese, German, Portugese, Romanian, Spanish and Swedish translations.

I will bring back the captives of My people Israel; they shall build the waste cities and inhabit them; they shall plant vineyards and drink wine from them; they shall also make gardens and eat fruit from them. I will plant them in their land, and no longer shall they be pulled up from the land I have given them," says the Lord your God.
Amos 9:14-15 (NKJV)

Probe leads to charges

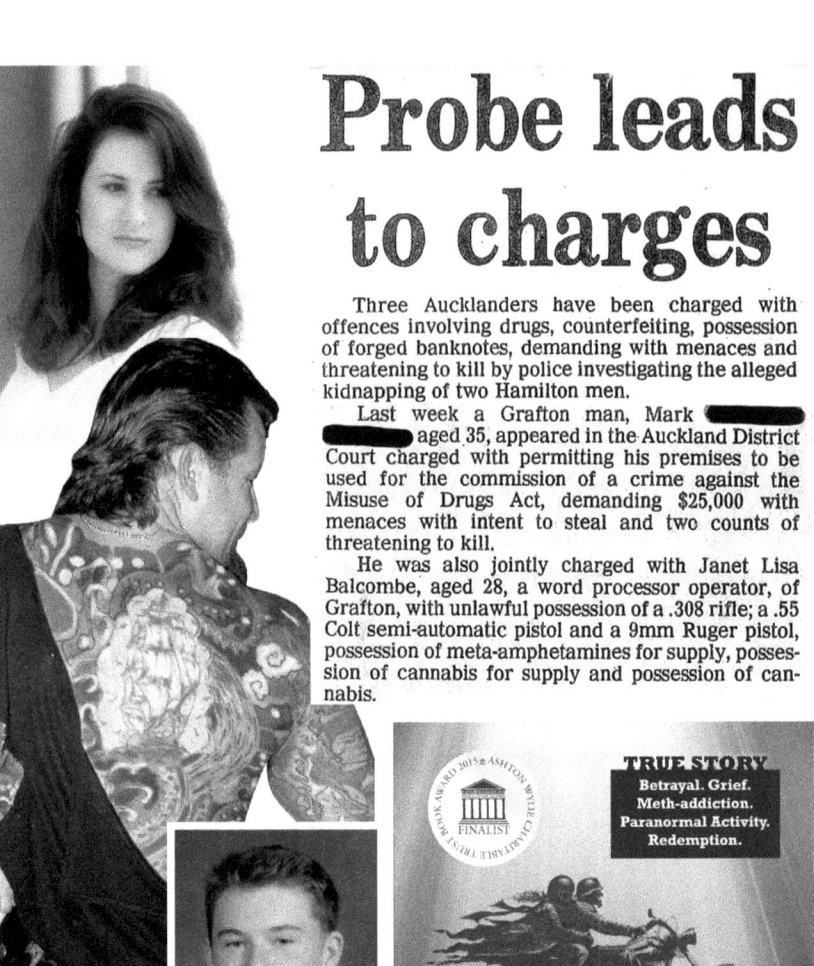

Three Aucklanders have been charged with offences involving drugs, counterfeiting, possession of forged banknotes, demanding with menaces and threatening to kill by police investigating the alleged kidnapping of two Hamilton men.

Last week a Grafton man, Mark ███████ aged 35, appeared in the Auckland District Court charged with permitting his premises to be used for the commission of a crime against the Misuse of Drugs Act, demanding $25,000 with menaces with intent to steal and two counts of threatening to kill.

He was also jointly charged with Janet Lisa Balcombe, aged 28, a word processor operator, of Grafton, with unlawful possession of a .308 rifle; a .55 Colt semi-automatic pistol and a 9mm Ruger pistol, possession of meta-amphetamines for supply, possession of cannabis for supply and possession of cannabis.

Top: Janet (25)　　*Middle*: Mark　　*Inset*: Roq (16)
Bottom: Ray & Janet Curle　　Memoir, The Wild Side, Ashton Wylie Literary Award Finalist

JANET BALCOMBE

Inside the mind of a wild child

How does a girl from a good family become a convicted kidnapper and meth survivor? Well, the kidnapping was just a misunderstanding. I was a good girl, guilty by association! *Mostly.*

I didn't plan to blast meth into my arm for two years. I didn't plan to go out with a meth cook — he became one over the eleven years we were together. It was just as well he wasn't a murderer, or an AIDS or Hepatitis victim. Plenty of others aren't so lucky. I didn't plan to spend twenty years off my face to kill my pain. But it was just as well that Jesus Christ turned out to be who He said He was, or there would have been no happy ever-after.

> In failing to plan, I'd planned to fail. Still, sitting in jail on a raft of charges including kidnapping, guns, drugs and counterfeiting was a little disappointing.

Why hadn't I planned my life? Well, I'd given up on myself by the time I had left school. I believed the lies they told about me, those ones I called my friends. I was no good, unacceptable and unaccepted.

If I turned my heart to stone and built a wall around it, it wouldn't hurt anymore because I didn't care. Except when my brother died. My stone-heart sure felt that, and another layer of concrete went up.

I turned to the easy crowd. They weren't hard to impress and accepted me with open arms. After falling in love, I found out he was married. By twenty-four I was a drug-addict and an adulteress. A home-wrecker.

My extreme make-under was complete. From career-girl to junkie. We were full-time outlaws. Meth addiction turned me into a user. A user of people — just like it does to all addicts in the end. You turn up at your mates' door with the eyes of a predator. Have they got any gear? No? *Ok, let's go.* They'd turn up at ours with the same look in their eyes.

I hadn't liked the person I was before, but I detested the person I'd become. My toxic relationship slowly squeezed the life out of my close relationships until I was isolated from my support system.

The black spiritual doors that my fascination with the occult and drug use had opened really were something else again. Psychotic and demonised, malnourished and paranoid, I was desperately unhappy and completely lost.

By grace I saw God contend with the demonic as it sought to contend with me while still in my sin. The demonic visitor that possessed my partner one dark night at the tattoo studio where we lived abhorred me. It saw that I was completely oblivious to the angelic protection that held it at bay as an intercessor prayed for me.

If this wasn't rock bottom, it would certainly do until I got there. But sadly, I still had a long way to go. In and out of jail, eventually my partner's drug-dealing morphed into cooking Meth for two Auckland gangs. Inevitably things turned bad.

> "Well, we can expect a visit," Mark said calmly one day. "I've got a loaded gun under my pillow but I won't use it because I don't care anymore."

'Neither do I,' I thought to myself. Suddenly my one year-old son and I both got sick. Very sick. Campylobacter. I fought as long as I could but eventually we had to go to my parent's place to recuperate for a few days. So I thought. But God had tricked me and we ended up never going back. Why? I surrendered my stone-heart to Jesus the living Christ. How on earth did it happen? Not without one hell of a fight!

Back at my parents place, unable to walk unaided, I looked at my reflection and saw the mask of death looking back at me. I'd had no idea how close I was. A few days later I realised I was blowing it; this thing called life, and cried out to God.

"God if you're real you'd better show up now or I'll go back!"

He showed up a couple of days later with a terrible vision, with my son's eternal destiny hanging in the balance. He showed the spiritual reality of my life without Him. It was ugly, and it was the first time I'd been properly scared in my entire life. Terrified.

It was only then that I accepted an invitation to a prayer meeting with my mother that night and there I accepted Christ. My walk on the wild side had just begun.

> After two weeks of relentless battery from hell I got the message. The enemy of my soul was not pleased. I learned the power of the name of Jesus and the power of His blood. I learned the power of praise and worship; and kept my eyes on Jesus, not Satan and his antics.

I began to experience true repentance and forgiveness. I had an insatiable hunger for the things of God; His word, prayer and worship.

Over time, God healed my heart and over two years, did many miracles restoring my shambolic affairs, including erasing a $26,000 tax bill. I learned who God is and who I was, at an intense six-month residential Certificate of Evangelism course at *Lifeway College* in New Zealand. This was extreme bible college with army flavour... boot-camp, parade, drill and PT.

I petitioned God for many years to bring me a husband and then He gave me a prophetic word.

"Nothing will happen for you in this area until you accept Jesus as your husband. Then you will be like royalty to Me."

I didn't care about finding a husband anymore in light of the promise that I would be like royalty to Him. What more could be better than that? But I didn't know what it meant to accept Jesus as my husband and decided to find out what it meant, or how to do it, and so I asked God to show me. He led me on a journey of discovery and by the time I had fully accepted Him as my husband I didn't want a natural husband anymore. I was now free from my own humanness, my own agenda, free to do His will and I set about writing my memoir, *Take a Walk on the Wild Side*.

A few years later I visited my home church one weekend. There just happened to be a visiting team from a large US prophetic ministry at the tiny country church. They pointed me out and said,

"This day is for you. Jesus is here to see you. He is your husband. He is coming down the aisle to see you. You need to dream bigger" [abridged version]

I was completely overcome with Jesus' glory and His love.

Finally, after thirteen years of being single and celibate God has brought me a husband. He is the son of *Youth for Christ* NZ's first evangelist, George Curle. He is one of the founding members of Promise Keepers in New Zealand and was campaign manager for international evangelist Bill Subritzky for thirteen years. I think he is royalty in Gods' kingdom.

When I realised who Ray was, I totally freaked. But I heard God say to my heart, *"Hey, remember what I said? When you have accepted Jesus as your husband, you will be like royalty to me."*

I clearly saw how God led his blind child by ways she had not known, and He's never stopped surprising me. He is taking me from platform to platform for His glory, speaking and ministering in healing and deliverance (exorcism) together with Ray. Together we are seeing people set free from addictions and other bondages, and bringing hope to the hopeless.

If he can do this for me, he can do it for you, your friends and your family. We need to dream bigger.

One of those platforms God has given me is writing for *Christian Life* news magazine. You are reading the first compilation of these true stories stories, and the second book in the series, *Radical Lives Vol II* is in the pipeline. I have another book to write as well, unpacking *The Wild Side* for those who want to know more. My re-titled memoir, *The Wild Side,* is available wherever books are sold.

You can contact Janet via **janet@wildsidepublishing.com** and visit **wildsidepublishing.com.** Janet is on Facebook.

Behold, I give you the authority to trample on serpents and scorpions, and over all the power of the enemy, and nothing shall by any means hurt you.
Luke 10:19 (NKJV)

EXCERPT FROM THE WILD SIDE

I gloomily watched our place in Symonds Street pass by through the paddy wagon portal and arrived at my new home, Mount Eden Prison, still in my best dress and high heels. The butch old guard gave me the once-over. *"Well, you can't wear that in here!"* she said, shaking her head. The things some people wear to jail these days. *No idea.*

"Oh sorry, shall I go home and get changed?" I asked. I'd love to go home. And stay home. I wanted to undo this whole thing. Undo, undo, undo, undo! Oh how I wished Mark had done the delivery that day and not me. I wish, I wish, if only this, if only that. I wished my stupid life away.

My clothes and shoes stored away in a brown paper bag, I was treated to a bath with parasite shampoo, lest I contaminate the prisoners. Dressed in a clean set of prison couture, I clutched my small bag of creature comforts; toothbrush, toothpaste, comb and soap. I was ready to meet my new mates.

"Follow me!" Butch barked. Heart thumping loudly, I followed the she-man into a new realm. Progress was slow, stopping every few metres to unlock and lock gates on the way to the remand wing. My internal critic offered harsh narrative and rarely paused for breath. The 'girls' didn't acknowledge me as I was let into their cage. My cell nestled underneath spaghetti junction. The city's aorta pumped people about their business twenty-four seven as my world shrank around me like plastic wrap. A gate clanging in the distance had the last word. There was nothing I could do that I needed to do. No one to see that I wanted to see. I ventured out of my cell, preferring the possibility of being torn to shreds by rabid inmates than my own company.

"Hi," I said, mustering a sheepish smile. Nobody smiled back; nobody spoke. Well, clearly behaviour like that wasn't tolerated. I decided to drink a cup of concrete and harden up. My esteemed company included an arsonist, a dope-grower from up north, and a heroin addict punk with a large tattoo around her neck that screamed ALEX in neo-Nazi script. ALEX had no trouble getting gear in the big house.

Top and bottom left:
Koebi and Steve Hart

Bottom right:
Steve when they first met

KOEBI HART

One straight shooter's journey from abuse and addiction to heaven and restoration

Every now and then God pulls a fast one and you slam straight into it. You didn't see it coming and you just can't pick yourself up and carry on like nothing happened. Meeting Koebi Hart was one such event. She is surely one of God's secret weapons. Koebi looks like a normal person but walks in supernatural grace because she gives supernatural grace to others, non-stop. She has a message for us. But first, a little back-story...

From a middle-class family, Koebi's Pakeha father wouldn't let her acknowledge her mother's Maori heritage. A sickly child, she suffered severe asthma attacks almost to the point of death before she would be reluctantly taken to the hospital. Speaking and laughing was unacceptable behaviour punished with beatings.

Bullied at home, she paid it forward at school until there wasn't a school left in Auckland who would take her. Rejected by her father, peers and the system, she attempted suicide at age nine, sexually active at ten, and taking drugs at twelve.

Desperately unhappy at home and with no safe place to go, she attempted suicide again at fourteen, but just as in the first attempt she heard the audible voice of God say, *"NO!"* and put the pills away. She fell pregnant and began living with a man she barely knew after being kicked out of home. Koebi's lifestyle was unsafe for her son who eventually went and lived with her mother.

When Koebi began working for the NZ Navy as a Civilian Stewardess, drug-use, depression and suicide were still regular companions. Desperate, she cried out one day, "God if you're real there's got to be someone out there for me." Koebi saw the word 'HART' in front of her eyes like a neon sign for twenty-four hours. Then she forgot all about it.

In 1985 Koebi was convicted of possession to supply Cannabis and received nine months periodic detention. Wanting to make a new start, she moved to Taranaki, but defaulted back to drugs and began associating with various groups including the Black Power.

> Then she met someone. But in a small town dates with a cop don't go unnoticed. Gang members killed her German Shepherd, and threw his body in front of her place as a calling card. "You'll be next."

She had a choice to make: drugs and a life of crime, or the good man. The moment she chose the cop, her future husband Steve HART (notice the last name), God removed her desire for drugs.

Steve and Koebi moved to Patea in the late 1980s, into the previous house of a Police officer who was also a Spirit-filled Christian and church Elder. In Koebi's brokenness she became such a disgusting drunk that Steve gave up drinking. She abused him verbally to the extreme, even threatening to run him over with the car — rejection seeking to sabotage her relationship before she could be rejected.

One month after they moved into the Christian's house, God took Koebi, still an unbeliever, to heaven. No, she didn't die — she doesn't know if she was in her body or out.

> "The whole atmosphere in heaven is filled with His presence. On the golden footpath the Lord, the light of the world, was consumed in light. We communicated by thought."

"He would hear my thoughts and I could hear his thoughts. He sent out rays of light to me. The first ray hit me in the heart which was LOVE like I'd never experienced. "Where is this love on earth?" I asked. "In my people," He said. "But I must say, it's sometimes hard to find His love in His people", she says.

"He sent another ray of light to me which was PEACE; the peace that surpasses all understanding. All of my life I longed for peace. The third ray was JOY, and I heard the Lord belly-laughing. I began to laugh and laugh because when I was a child I couldn't laugh. For the first time I was truly happy. I saw a carpet of purple flowers on either side of the footpath."

"Why are there purple flowers, Lord?"

"Because of my royalty."

Koebi was overwhelmed with just how much Jesus loves her. She didn't want to leave his presence. She didn't want to leave the love, joy, and peace. But the Lord said to her that she must go back. Back on planet earth she was overcome with an awesome fear of the Lord and the reality of knowing God was real. She couldn't stop her body from shaking.

"It was like heaven was shaking hell out of me."

She couldn't adjust her eyes to the room in her house. Everything looked hard and harsh because of heaven's glory. From that moment she couldn't swear and the desire for alcohol had gone. The Holy Spirit taught her a new vocabulary and He taught her to read. At school she had been in a special-needs reading group and had struggled to string words together.

Steve had his own encounter with the Lord the same night Koebi was in heaven. But being very intellectual, Steve's head got in the way and God had to smoke some of his false beliefs about scientific beginnings.

Because Koebi had been a blasphemer, she didn't know how to tell Steve what had happened to her. She said, "I've been blessed by God". He said, *"I know you have,"* and told her what had happened to him. For the first time since childhood he had prayed a prayer about a tree in their back yard that attracted wasps, a problem, as he is fatally allergic to stings. "Lord, I know you can do something about this tree."

The next morning the tree was flat on the ground with the roots cut clean away, having fallen silently on a still night with no vibration. It missed the clothesline, woodshed, garage and house. The Inspector of Police asked, "Who cut the tree down? You needed to get permission."

"We prayed and God did it."

"Oh whatever you do, don't pray for me!" he said with a smile.

It was 1990 and Koebi and Steve still weren't Christians. Koebi went to a Presbyterian church where they had an altar call. The Lord moved Koebi's legs without her moving them because she wasn't going forward. Koebi had cursed Steve so much the Lord said she had to bless him and speak life into his spirit. Steve attended a Bill Subritzky meeting six months later, because the change in her was so dramatic – like night and day. He responded to the altar call. The policeman whose house they had moved into was on the team at that night, and prayed for him.

Steve was so filled with the Spirit that he couldn't speak or walk straight for three hours.

God had begun a mighty work of restoration in their lives. Koebi began Bible study and theological training, and became an ordained Anglican minister. Over time, God healed damage to Koebi's brain from drug-abuse. Eventually, after twenty-five years, God spoke to her in a vision and called her out of the Anglican church.

Koebi and Steve had a daughter. As a young child she stopped going to Sunday School because she needed more mature teaching. She regularly saw angels and even massaged Jesus' feet. Then disaster struck. In her teens, Koebi's daughter was viciously raped by someone who was known to the family. She was different after that. Koebi's daughter had left the building. She cut off her glorious long hair, got piercings and dressed dark. She wouldn't accept ministry and was physically abusive to her father. A three-year walk in the dark for the family had just begun.

Koebi prayed and prayed for her daughter but saw no change. Rage bubbled just under the surface of Koebi's heart and erupted each time she saw her daughter's rapist. Even as an ordained minister, she couldn't stop herself flooring the accelerator to run him over if she saw him crossing the street. Then one day she saw him sitting out front of her shop on a park bench. Her rage exploded and she grabbed the biggest carving knife she could find.

"He's not even going to know what hit him!" she said to herself and headed towards the door. Then God intervened.

He took her legs out from under her and down on the floor she screamed and screamed until her rage was gone for good. The Spirit of God spoke to her, saying,

> "But I forgave YOU. But I forgave YOU. But I forgave *YOU*," over and over again until she got it. She forgave her daughter's rapist and was set free.

Still, her daughter was in darkness. One night after three years of watching her daughter slip further away, Koebi stood outside her daughter's room and cried out to God. *"God, I don't know what to say to You anymore. I don't know what to pray anymore. I've prayed every prayer I can pray. Where is my daughter? Her body is in there, but that's not her! WHERE IS SHE?"*

In a vision, God showed Koebi walking into the darkness, and finding her daughter's hand. She put a backpack down and stepped back into the light with her daughter. "God, what was in the backpack?" she asked. God said, *"It's a bomb."* He revealed that the bomb was made up of Scripture. Koebi fasted and prayed for three days to download the Scriptures she needed to make the bomb, and placed them under her daughter's mattress. The day the bomb was laid was the day her daughter returned, and began her long journey back.

Koebi's forgiveness was tested while out shopping one day when she ran face to face into the rapist. *"I know what you did to my daughter,"* she said. He was terrified... *"But I forgive you."*

Later Koebi saw the rapist's mother who was unaware of what her son had done. *"How is your son?"* Koebi asked. "Not good," the mother replied. "He's got agoraphobia and hasn't been out of the house for two years." Koebi replied, *"If you would like, I could visit him or arrange for a male priest to call on him."* Koebi's willingness to help the man was evidence that her heart was truly healed.

Koebi's story is large and she shoots from the hip. There is much more, but it'll have to wait until next time. She has shown us the power of true forgiveness and earned the right to encourage us in this. Koebi is now an international evangelist; her ministry is called *Straight Street Ministries*. It's amazing what God can do with one broken life. If He can do it for Koebi, He can do it for anyone.

You can contact Koebi on **7straightstreet@gmail.com**

Top: Matthew Needham *(end right)* and family
Left: Matthew at Bill Subritzky's 90th birthday celebration
Right: Memoir, *To Live or to Die*

MATTHEW NEEDHAM

From teen street evangelist to a man on a mission

The enemy knew who Matthew was well before he did, and tried hard to shut him down before he found out. I mean who becomes a street and nightclub evangelist at sixteen years old? Matthew Needham, that's who.

Suicide stalked Matthew in his teenage years, but the Lord kept him safe for an encounter with Him by the power of the Holy Spirit, which irrevocably changed his life. When I bumped into Matthew at Bill Subritzky's 90th birthday celebration, I saw a rare purity shining out of him and understood where his power comes from. The pure in heart see God.

Matthew was brought up in a small farming community of about forty families in Northland, New Zealand. There was a primary school, a social hall, a church, and that was pretty much the size of it. All their shopping was done at a near-by village or other not so near-by places. Matthew and his siblings were picked up for school by bus from outside their gate. When he first entered that school he remembers being frightened by some of the older boys who were twice his age and, it seemed, twice his size. Two of them made him bow down in front of them and kiss their shoes – a precursor to eventually being severely and systematically bullied. When he was about age eleven, it became harder to get along with some of the other students because of his faith, and he was seriously harrassed for believing in God.

There were two different sides to Matthew's life; the happy home life – doing things on the farm that he enjoyed, with a faith in God that couldn't be shaken, and a life at school where he was being crushed by bullying and just didn't know how to overcome the darkness of this world. Held in bondage by fear he had no idea how to get out of it. The weaknesses in his life had opened the door for the devil to attack. Sometimes he felt like he was trapped by life's circumstances and began to think, *"What is the point of living like this?"*

> A stronghold built up in Matthew's mind, that whenever something went wrong, he would think about taking his life. The devil used this to make him think that his life was worthless. Eventually a Spirit of Death that had been given a legal right to be there, was always calling him to die.

At the end of a particularly hard week, someone abused him verbally and it was the last straw. He decided he had to get out of this world and determined in his mind that when he got home from school he would end it all. Grabbing the rifle from the back of his parent's wardrobe, Matthew climbed out the back window where he fell on his knees, looked up to Heaven and said a last prayer,

"O God, please forgive me for what I am about to do. Don't hold this sin against me, but Lord God, I can't live on this earth."

> "I loaded a bullet into the gun, put the barrel of the gun in the middle of my forehead and put my finger on the trigger. I closed my eyes and quickly pulled the trigger to blow my brains out. But the gun didn't fire. Nothing happened."

The gun didn't fire because the safety lock had been on, unbeknown to him. Matthew had fully expected it to fire, and if the safety lock hadn't been on, he would have died right there. He burst out in tears because he wasn't dead. As he was crying, he became too afraid to attempt killing himself a second time, so, picking up the gun, Matthew climbed back inside through the window, and put the gun back in the wardrobe. Maybe the crying had helped relieve his distressed state, and he didn't really want to die now after all. What he really wanted was a greater purpose to live.

In due course Matthew's parents moved to the outskirts of Whangarei and he went to a weekend camp organised by the youth group of the new church they attended. The guest speaker was sharing his testimony about how God had saved his life. Although this guy had been a bit of a gangster with some involvement with drugs and crime, and a lot of alcohol, God had saved him in a dramatic way. He had a powerful testimony and Matthew was getting desperate for his message to finish so he could go forward. He needed prayer urgently!

"As soon as the call for prayer was given I rushed to the front. I didn't know anything about the anointing or the presence of the Holy Spirit at that time, but I was immediately in the presence of God. I started to cry, and it was the deepest I had ever cried in my whole life."

In 1991 at just sixteen, Matthew stepped out in faith to lead the life of a street evangelist, traveling through his home country witnessing in the streets, outside nightclubs and in any church that opened the door to him.

Matthew had still not been water baptised during the time when he was street evangelizing. For a couple of years he had been convicted to do this, but had not been brave enough to take that step. All his excuses fell away after being baptised with the Holy Spirit, but it still took nearly five months before he was finally baptised in water in December, 1990.

After six years of street evangelism he left for his first overseas missions trip to Fiji. At the end of 1996, a second call to the mission field came and in 1999 Matthew began evangelism among Muslims in Africa. In 2003 the Lord called him a third time to leave everything and preach the Gospel. This time it was to the Hindus, Muslims and Buddhists of India and Nepal.

More recently Matthew has been working for the Lord in the East African countries of Kenya and Uganda.

In November 2015 Matthew returned to Fiji to set up a new ministry and marry his beautiful Fiji Indian bride.

Matthew's memoir, *To Live or To Die* is well worth reading and is available on **Amazon.com**

You can contact Matthew by visiting **evangelistmatthew.com**

I will build My church, and the gates of Hades shall not prevail against it.
Matthew 16:18 (NKJV)

Top:
Norm McLeod in his Gizzy hood

Right:
Norm, back in the day

NORM MCLEOD

The warrior pastor who knows no limits

Thank God for the guy who told Norm McLeod that *"One day, in the deepest darkest moment of your life, you're going to need to call on the name of Jesus – and He will help you."*

That guy was Norm's best mate, ex-pimp and drug dealer turned Jesus freak – and this was that day. Overdosing and paralysed, Norm lay facedown, drowning in a pool of his own vomit. He was in trouble. His mouth and one nostril were submerged and his remaining nostril would soon be blocked, as he couldn't stop vomiting.

Norm didn't believe in God or Satan, but in what seemed to be the closing moments of his life, his world-view was about to be severely rocked. He heard footsteps approaching and willed them to stop and help him; to roll him over so that he could breathe. The footsteps did stop. However what he heard as the person laughed at him, was straight from the pit of hell... **"I've got you this time!"**

At that moment he knew beyond a shadow of a doubt that Satan and hell were real – and that's where he was headed right now.

Norm had seen his best mate's life totally transformed by a miracle healing and had heard all about his Jesus. Norm was happy for him, but wasn't ready for religion. He was enjoying his lifestyle of sex, drugs and rock 'n roll.

> But Norm's deepest, darkest moment had arrived. He couldn't call out with his mouth because it was literally submerged in vomit, so he cried out to Jesus in his mind, with all his heart, "JESUS, HELP ME!"

Instantly his head stopped spinning and the vomiting ceased. It took an hour for the paralysis to subside and finally he was able to get up and slowly but surely make his way home.

Norm had grown up in Oamaru, his father European, his mother Maori. In spite of a loving family background, the biker lifestyle, along with violence and martial arts, had sunk their claws deeply into him. Norm knew Jesus had saved him that terrible day – but it wasn't until 1979, two years later that he and his wife Jess, totally dedicated their lives to Him. For the next ten years Norm served under Pastor John Ballantyne in Oamaru until receiving a supernatural mandate to go to Gisborne and start a warrior church.

In 1989 the Spirit of God, suspended him in mid air over Poverty Bay – a place he had neither been to or seen, took Norm up in an open vision. As he looked down he saw many unmanned waka (Maori war canoes) sitting still on the shimmering sea.

He heard the audible voice of God say to him, "You will come to this place and raise up for Me a warrior church." As he heard the Lord's voice he saw people coming up out of the earth as he spoke of Christ to them, and they went and took their places in the waka.

The Lord's voice continued, *"When it is time I will send these waka forth by the wind of My Spirit into the city, the coast, the nation and to distant shores of other lands. These waka will take My warriors who will share My message of hope in My power."* Then Norm saw the fully manned waka moving into the places that God's voice commanded them to go.

In 1991 Norm and Jess moved to Gisborne in obedience to God. They knew no one, but when they planted the *House of Breakthrough,* it grew strongly. There were new converts from the first service attendance of 31, to 500 in the first four years.

Revival and miraculous signs and wonders followed them right from the start with a girl healed of AIDs. Tumours and cancers were healed, arthritics walked into services with sticks – and walked out without them. Abuse victims, addicts, gang members and the broken, flocked into the presence of God and received healing and salvation.

The church's phenomenal growth and involvement in helping gang members find a better way of life caught the attention of national television that featured them on TVNZ programmes *(Assignment* and *Extreme Close Up).*

As God promised, he gave them the nations as well. Over the last two and a half decades Norm and Jess have led ministry teams nationally and internationally. Many of the team members are people who were once captives but are now free of addictions, fears and dysfunction and now encourage and help others find freedom in Christ.

Kapa Haka and healing teams have gone out from the House of Breakthrough to Fiji, Vanuatu, Cambodia, Malaysia, India, Austria, Germany, Switzerland, Slovakia, the United States and England.

> Today, *House of Breakthrough* churches in India are experiencing ongoing revival in the supernatural manifest presence of God, resulting in thousands coming to Christ.

Norm and Jess equip, empower and deploy God's people to go beyond just academic theology and operate in "realogy." This year alone Norm has ministered in Chile, Fiji, Australia, Pakistan, India and Singapore, seeing thousands saved and hundreds of God's people encouraged, empowered and deployed.

From one extreme to the other, Norm and Jess have been serving God now for thirty-six years. So thank God for Norm's mate! *Let's be that guy.* The one who tells someone else the one thing that will save his or her life.

That Jesus saves.

You can find **House of Breakthrough Tairawhiti** on Facebook.

For whoever calls on the name of the Lord shall be saved.
Rom 10:13 (NKJV)

Top: Phil and Rowena Paikea
Left: From Black Power to God power *(Phil on ground)*
Right: Phil *(on the right)* in the company of a few good men

PHIL PAIKEA

One of God's generals leading from the front with his boots firmly on the ground

I couldn't help see the correlation between the dramas playing out in real life, and the spiritual drama that rages every day for our souls. Standing at my mate's committal, the crematorium fire roared in our ears and I braced myself for the inevitable flowery speel from the minister at the Mongrel Mob funeral. I loved my mate; he was an awesome guy. However, it takes more than that to get to heaven.

Jesus said, "I am the way, the truth, and the life. No one comes to the Father except through Me.
John 14:6 (NKJV)

I was in for a surprise. The minister was ex-hardman Phil Paikea. He spoke truth in love to the heavily tattooed crowd with a concise five-minute gospel message that ended with a challenge. It was refreshing to hear him say, that although my friend had lived for himself, he hoped he'd been given a chance to accept Jesus in the closing moments of his life.

Part Maori, part Irish is a volatile mix. Phil grew up in Helensville in a two-parent family but suffered violent discipline and ran away at age fifteen. After working in forestry, then living the street life, he went to Christchurch and his crime career began with gang members.

On the run from police in 1977, Phil landed in Whangarei where, with a group of mates and family members, he helped establish Whangarei Black Power in 1979. It wasn't long before he became President.

Then he met the future Mrs Rowena Paikea. Eventually she tired of the gang lifestyle: cops turning up at their home, gang members coming and going, and issued an ultimatum — Phil chose the boys. Rowena left with their daughter. In time the penny dropped and he left the gang and won his family back.

In 1987 Rowena gave her heart to Christ at a Luis Palau crusade in Whangarei, and The Hound of Heaven wooed Phil through the change in her – (her love and unconditional acceptance) and the friendship and perseverance of Rowena's pastor, Mike Norman. One day Phil found himself completely undone on Mike's floor, repenting and surrendering to God. He felt he was floating as a huge weight lifted off him and he got straight into evangelism.

Two weeks after surrendering to Christ, Phil had a near-death experience through drowning. Semi-conscious after being revived, God showed Phil a vision of his calling and destiny – ministering to gang members.

> As Phil was dying he called out to God, *"Father, receive my spirit!"* Instantly, he was in a very dark, cold place. He tried to touch his face with his hand but his hand went right through it. Voices screamed, *"Let me out!"* and another voice said, *"Shut up! You deserve to be here!"*

Phil's teeth started nashing, he began weeping uncontrollably as spoken of in the Scriptures,

> But the sons of the kingdom will be cast out into outer darkness. There will be weeping and gnashing of teeth.
> **Matthew 8:12 (NKJV)**

Phil felt a fear like he had never experienced before, and says this experience always serves as a backstop whenever he is tempted, as he never wants to risk being in that place ever again.

Then, still in the vision, he saw a row of Maori warriors doing a Haka on the rocks. He started speaking what sounded like an ancient Maori language but Phil thinks he could have been speaking in tongues. Phil saw a small light that got bigger and bigger, then it fell on his face. He saw himself standing back to back with Mike Norman, surrounded by patched gang members, who were in turn surrounded by angels.

In 1988 Phil was baptised and married Rowena. She wanted to bury the old man and marry the new man on the same day. Phil built a solid foundation, spending time in church and completing the *Lifeway College* First Wave Army training.

> One day Jesus said to Phil, *"Follow Me"* and then He walked right outside the church. He followed Jesus out the door and into the community of Ruakaka Village. He has been there ever since on his journey of redemption, putting back what he took from the community, where he was one of the original drug dealers.

Phil has worked with youth, started a social service and together with Rowena, runs a foster home and have fostered over 180 foster children. Phil was involved in organising the *White Ribbon Ride* to create national awareness of family violence, which has since taken on a life of its own.

In January 2015, after twenty years of being violence, drug and alcohol-free, Phil joined two existing speakers and champions for the national *R U OK* anti-violence against women and children campaign.

But in all of this, he has things in the right order: his relationship with God comes first, then his relationship with his wife and family, and then his ministry comes last. Because of this, God blesses all of these things. Phil and Rowena have been together for over thirty-six years (married for twenty-seven), have five daughters, one son and seven grandchildren, and over 180 foster children. That's no small feat.

> "I used to ride an unbridled fast stallion. It would race here and there and cover a lot of ground. But I realised in the hurry I was missing a lot of things God was doing. Now I ride a donkey, nice and slow. But a donkey carries a heavier load," says Phil.

Phil Paikea is on Facebook if you would like to make contact.

Top:
A storm leaves Radio Hauraki's pirate ship, *Tiri,* blown on shore at Waipu Cove, NZ

Bottom left: Ray's cheesy studio shot when he had hair

Bottom right: Ray and Janet Curle at Bill Subritzky's 90 birthday celebration

RAY CURLE

From pirate to preacher

I'll let you in on a little secret. My author name is Janet Balcombe but my real name is now Janet Curle. Little did I know that when a stranger approached me to buy my book one day, we would end up married. Nothing short of an act of God could have connected these two radicals.

Being the son of a well-known evangelist brought with it certain expectations: for example, going to Sunday school, Bible class and church. But there was rebellion hiding in Ray's heart, so as a teenager rock music and surfing became his escape hatch.

At age nineteen, Ray joined Auckland's pirate station *Radio Hauraki* as an ad salesman and copywriter. They transmitted from a coastal freighter in the Hauraki Gulf, near Great Barrier Island.

This boat was the *Tiri*, the star of the film, *3 Mile Limit*.

At age twenty, Ray sailed to Australia with two friends in a 32-foot sloop, *The Orbiter*, and surfed the East Coast. Then after a year, he went back to rejoin *Radio Hauraki* who now had a legal licence to broadcast and were based in Caltex House in Auckland. London called a couple of years later and he moved to the UK and worked for *Thames Television*. From there he went to the first private FM radio station in the UK, *Capital Radio*.

At age twenty-four Ray married his Auckland girlfriend and returned to New Zealand for the birth of his daughter, Amanda. He formed *Creative Media Services* and picked up the sales representation for four private radio stations, including Hauraki. But this was the 1970s and sex, drugs and rock'n'roll ruled. Excessive Marijuana consumption and the occasional fling with Cocaine led to a marriage split. Ray left on his own to manage *Radio Otago* (4XO) in Dunedin, working with Mike Baker at *Radio Central* in Alexandra.

On a trip to Auckland to sort out the separation details, Ray's then six year old daughter began weeping as she realised her parents were serious about living apart. Ray says, *"Something like a guitar string snapped inside my heart."* Later he read in the Bible that in the last days God will turn the hearts of the fathers back to the children and the children's hearts toward their fathers. Ray immediately turned back to the Lord that he knew as a child and made the move back to Auckland.

He was invited to be Sales Director of 89 Stereo FM (the first private station to get a FM licence in NZ), and whilst in the boardroom preparing the application papers, he got a call terminating his marriage. That day his mind was in turmoil, and when he got home, he lay on his bed asking the Lord for forgiveness for every sin he could remember committing.

Then something miraculous happened.

> "As I cried out to the Lord an incredible thing happened. I was suddenly charged with what seemed like a zillion volts of electricity that transfixed me to the bed so that I was unable to move. For what seemed like an eternity, wave after wave of God's love flowed right through me."

"I'd had some euphoric drug trips in my life-time, but nothing compared to this amazing experience."

If he wasn't born-again before, he certainly was now – and well and truly baptised in the Holy Spirit and Fire.

After resigning from 89 Stereo FM, Ray worked for Universal Homes and set up a branch in Taupo. There he met Roy Waldrom who mentored him for two years and taught him to hear the voice of the Lord. While he was there, Ray's daughter came to live with him and he became a solo dad for five years.

Returning to Auckland he met a lovely Christian lady who had also been a solo parent with a daughter, Angie. This led to twenty years of marriage and four amazing children were added to the clan: Sam, Rebekah, Rachel and Jonny.

> For thirteen years, Ray was the Crusade Manager for New Zealand's most well known evangelists, Bill and Pat Subritzky, and helped to organise national and international crusades.

Leading the deliverance counselling at Bill's Auckland meetings, Ray witnessed God heal and deliver hundreds of people. He worked beside his brother, David, who developed the video production side of *Dove Ministries* and counted it a great privilege to be part of the original team who launched the men's ministry, *Promise Keepers NZ*.

Believing it was time to move on, Ray took his family to Gisborne and set up a tourism-marketing consultancy. One day he heard the Lord say, *"I'm calling you to preach and teach on the judgement of God. It is not a message of fire and brimstone, but of love and compassion."*

After four years he heard the Lord say move back to Auckland. Upon asking why he had been led to Gisborne in the first place, Ray believes the Lord said, *"To be broken and prepared for change."*

Those changes came thick and fast. Back in Auckland, Ray worked part-time for *DayStar* magazine and at the *Westpac* Bank call centre in Onehunga. He then became the advertising manager for *Initiate Media* representing Christian publications in Australia, and *Christian Life*, the New Zealand monthly news magazine.

Unfortunately, with much heartache, Ray experienced his second marriage failure, but always hoped and prayed for reconciliation. In 2013 he underwent triple-bypass surgery. While in the hospital a sister-in-law called from London with a prophetic word containing three specific topics:

"Hope deferred makes the heart sick. Keep looking at Me. Don't be anxious about your children. I love them far more than you do, and I'm already melting their hearts," and, *"The ministry I have called you to will happen in My time. Be patient."*

After repenting for his anxieties and sense of failure, Ray had total peace about the operation, and had a super fast recovery. After 9 years of being single and celibate, he met me... and God invited us to get married.

God is so radical. Although we live in a tiny country town, Ray sells advertising for a global network of magazines and websites. We work closely together as a team, sharing our testimonies in churches around the North Island, at *Full Gospel Business Men's Fellowship* dinners and local conferences.

The ministry God called Ray to (back in Gisborne) has finally begun. When Ray was age ten he had an impression from the Lord that he would be preaching in the last days before Jesus returned! This is now happening.

Ray can be contacted by email on **ray@wildsidedesign.net**

Believe on the Lord Jesus Christ, and you will be saved, you and your household.
Acts 16:31

Top:
Tawhiri and Katy Littlejohn and the babes

Bottom:
Tawhiri on drums

TAWHIRI LITTLEJOHN

From session drummer to pastor

So how exactly does one of New Zealand's top session drummers become a pastor at just age twenty-nine? Well it's quite a story so kick back and check it out. This is what total surrender looks like.

We met in Whangarei at a conference where I had been invited to share my testimony. When I met Tawhiri Matea Littlejohn I spotted the purity of his heart and his total surrender to Christ a mile off. When I heard that he was a pastor at such a young age, I knew there was a big story to be told.

He invited me to share with his flock at Kaiwaka Revival Church a few weeks later. When we arrived we found him totally at home behind the drums bringing some incredible beats during the worship. The surprises just kept coming!

Tawhiri was born in a very big hurry in the small Northland town of Kaiwaka. He had started how he meant to continue. Tawhiri Matea means 'God of the wind, thunder and lightning.' But like so many, his world was soon shattered when at age five, his parents split. Raised in the Ratana church, he lived with his Mum while his Dad, a full-time musician, continued touring.

From a young age the drums captivated Tawhiri. At age thirteen he went to live with his father who bought him his first drum kit. With little else to do in the small town, Tawhiri practiced endlessly. The drums made him happy and gave him a purpose. His dream of being a full-time session drummer was born. He was very disciplined in his practice routine and never wasted time or missed a day.

By age fourteen Tawhiri often toured with his father all over New Zealand. By eighteen he was playing for many different bands and artists, and then studied at Auckland's *MAINZ* Music School. Playing for King Kapisi was the start of a big break. His girlfriend Katy decided to leave him so he could pursue his music career. As a youngster Tawhiri always wanted to be popular in the music scene, party hard and hook up with girls. He was now free to pursue all of his desires and was living the life he'd always wanted. Until one night in a nightclub – something strange happened.

> Drunk and having a good time, Tawhiri suddenly felt a deep conviction fall upon him like a sword piercing his heart. This conviction just would not leave, and for the first time in his life, he felt very lost.

Tawhiri had given up smoking weed because it made him paranoid, but he got so bored while learning to play forty new songs for a band, he got stoned to make it go faster. As he lay in bed that night, still stoned, he began to think about his life. The conviction was still deep in his heart and he felt so empty.

"Then while I was lying in the dark thinking, I heard a voice say, *"Follow Me."* It was the Lord. When you hear His voice, you know without a doubt who is speaking. It was like a voice I'd always known, that I had always ignored. But for the first time I paid attention. From childhood I'd always known I was called as He had come to me in my dreams, and His power would come upon me in measures I haven't experienced to this day. But I would always deny Him as I didn't want Him. Well not yet anyway. First, I wanted to live my life the way I wanted to. Yet God chose to speak to me right when I was seeking to live out my sinful lifestyle.

So when I heard His voice I said to him as if He were standing right there, *"No, I will not follow You. Not now. I will follow You when I am an old man, that way I can do whatever I want now, and still get to heaven before I die."*

"Then another voice spoke to me, which was very seductive. It was the evil one, who said, *"Yes that's right. You can follow God and still have all you want."* He tempted me just like he tempted Jesus in the wilderness. Then the Lord showed me all the things I wanted and I said to Him, *"That's what I want, Jesus,"* and Jesus said to me again, *"Follow Me."*

"He said I had to give up everything I could see, as I could see in a vision all that the enemy wanted to give me. Everything in me was saying, *"No God! Why did you come to me now? Not now God!"* Then I saw a cross and Jesus said again, ***"If you want to follow me you must give up all you see now."*** This was hard. I didn't want to. But the conviction in my heart just wouldn't leave, and after many hours of battling I finally said, *"Okay Lord, I will give it a go. I will give up that other stuff."*

Instantly Tawhiri felt peace, and he was set free and born again with a deep heart of repentance and sorrow for the selfish life he had been living. His mind was freed and he now looked at the world through different eyes. He was even amazed at the beauty of all of God's creation, as if seeing it for the first time.

Tawhiri began to read the Bible and pray continually. He was hungry for God and spent the first six months in deep repentance.

He learned to live by faith and trusted in God for everything. As Tawhiri consecrated himself to the Lord he began to see amazing things happen. He got a call to play in the band *Sons of Zion*, began session playing with many others and started the band *Soljah*. He played with artists Hazardous, musicians from Ardijah, Annabel Faye, Peiter T, Dane Rumble, Stan Walker, Jay Williams and many others. The music scene really opened up for him and he was doing what he always wanted.

In the early years Tawhiri didn't join a church because he was always touring. Still he refused to be influenced by the lifestyle of drugs, drinking and sex and learned to walk with God and abide in His presence no matter where he was. But eventually, being immersed in the lifestyle began to make him feel depressed.

At the end of 2011, he took time out to fast and pray, to find out if it was the Lord's will for him to remain in the music scene — which it was. Tawhiri and Katy were reunited. They were married, moved back to Kaiwaka. The Lord blessed with their first baby and began going to church. 2012 saw Tawhiri on tour again with the summer season of music festivals, but was now strengthened by God's word. He was on a mission.

> "I was no longer concerned about fame or success. I just wanted God's will, to win souls for Jesus. From 2012 to 2014 I witnessed the most incredible demonstrations of God's power in night-clubs, at music festivals, in cars, in the green rooms, and back-stage with other bands."

Everywhere Tawhiri went, God went with him. Tawhiri was ready to move in God's power. He saw salvations, healings, and deliverances, and would move in the spiritual gifts of the word of knowledge and prophecy, that would instantly set people free from alcohol intoxication.

Many of the people who God sent to Tawhiri were back-slidden Christians, and His power would fall, more than one would normally see in a church service. Tawhiri preached sermons on music video sets and even had some of the camera crew give their hearts to the Lord. He witnessed some of the most powerful demonstrations of God's power delivering people from demonic possession, as people often spontaneously manifested around him.

> "I even witnessed God's protection over me in the music scene when I had drunk-people try to come violently against me, but as they came close, I felt a wall of the Holy Spirit envelop me. When they stepped into it they began to weep uncontrollably, not knowing what was happening to them."

Tawhiri understood then that the church is not a building, but God's people are His living temple, bringing His kingdom wherever they go. As Tawhiri played, he grieved over the condition of the people living in their sin and he would pray, *"God, when you say it's time, I am coming out of this, Lord. I am only here to do Your will."*

That day came in April 2014. Tawhiri was so happy and knew that he'd done his Father's will and a new leg of his journey was beginning. In 2015 he was ordained as a co-Pastor of *Kaiwaka Revival Church*. *"Jesus has changed my life and I owe it all to Him. My old life has gone and I am a new creation in Him."*

Tawhiri loves seeing God transform and restore lives and his community is experiencing a spiritual awakening. After playing in front of 40,000 people and fourteen years of touring, he now enjoys having time with his wife and kids. He does miss his friends in the music scene and prays the Lord will set them free, as He did for him.

> "I know how strong the hold of music is. It becomes everything in your life, even more important than family. It blinds you and leaves you always seeking success and never satisfyied. It is never able to fulfill that void in your heart. Only Jesus can."

"Nothing in all the world can ever compare to knowing Him and His great love for us. I'm excited at this adventure, and I am hungrier for Him now than ever before."

Tawhiri can be contacted on **tawhiri.l@gmail.com**

Then Jesus said to him, "Away with you, Satan! For it is written, 'You shall worship the Lord your God, and Him only you shall serve.'"
Matthew 4:10 (NKJV)

PRAYER

No one comes to the Father except through Me (Jesus Christ)

NEWSFLASH: We came from God (not monkeys — well most of us, anyway), were made perfectly equipped to fulfill the purpose for which we were created — to worship and glorify God with our hearts, lives and the gifts he has given us; and to spend eternity with him. The only problem is, since the fall of Adam, the sin ceiling tends to get in the way of our communication. God is holy, and we are not, until we take up the righteousness Jesus offers.

No matter how good we are or are not, we are all sinners, every last one of us. For *all have sinned and fall short of the glory of God (Romans 3:23)*. *The wages of sin is death, but the gift of God is eternal life through Christ Jesus our Lord (Romans 6:23)*. But God *demonstrates his own love for us in this: while we were still sinners, Christ died for us (Romans 5:8)*.

The Gospel means 'good news', and the good news is that your sins and mine have been paid for at the cross. You are the apple of his eye; the reason he lived and died and rose again.

We can't earn salvation by good works or deserve it by having good character. If this were the case, Jesus would have died for nothing. God offers it to us freely. All we have to do is receive it by faith.

If we confess with our mouth, *"Jesus is Lord,"* and believe in our heart that God raised him from the dead, we will be saved *(Romans 10:9)*. Everyone who calls on the name of the Lord will be saved *(Acts 2:21)*. If you're ready to give your life to Jesus, ask the same question I asked:

> "God, if you're real, show yourself to me."

You've got nothing to lose and everything to gain. If your heart is beating faster than normal, and you just know that you want Jesus to be the Lord of your life, pray this one:

> "Lord, I surrender my life to You. Come into my heart. I ask forgiveness for my sins. By faith I receive the gift of eternal life. I ask that You baptise me with Your Holy Spirit and with fire. Thank You for setting everything right between You and me. Show me the way forward with You, in Jesus' name, Amen."

Congratulations, you've just made the most important decision of your life. Now ask God to show you a good church to be a part of, and to bring the right people around you and angels to protect you, and He will.

The best is yet to come.

WILD SIDE PUBLISHING

Buy from wildsidepublishing.com, or anywhere books are sold.

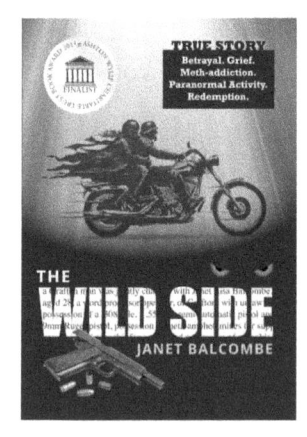

There is hope for the addicts, the rebels, and the broken-hearted.

Sitting in prison on a raft of charges including kidnapping, guns, drugs and counterfeiting was very different to the scenario Janet had envisaged for her life.

Previously published as, Take a Walk on the Wild Side. New cover, colour photos, same story.

Discover great life hacks straight from the heart's of these remarkable survivors.

15 true life stories you just won't be able to put down.

Get inside the head of a notorious armed-robber, a handful of gangsters and rebels, drug addicts, an IRA bomb survivor, a session drummer, and a serial entrepreneur for an unforgettable ride.

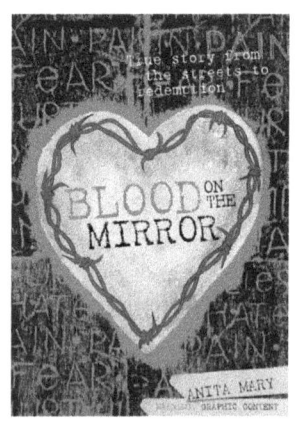

After a childhood of lies and abuse, emotional and physical violence, many different homes and 18 schools, Anita ran away to be 'free'.

What she encountered along the way was everything but freedom, until finally she made the wisest choice anyone could ever make...

absoluteartnz.com

---

wildsidepublishing.com

WSP

real stories. real hope.